SOMETIMES I'M SO HAPPY I'M NOT SAFE ON THE STREETS

DEAN WILSON

SOMETIMES I'M SO HAPPY I'M NOT SAFE ON THE STREETS

Dean Wilson

ISBN 9781903110331

First published in this edition 2016 by Wrecking Ball Press.

Copyright Dean Wilson

Cover design by humandesign.co.uk

Typeset by atomluft.com

CONTENTS

Mary · 9

Oak Vaults · 10

Hull Hath No Fury Like A Poet Scorned · 11

Sid · 12

Bad Penny · 13

Metal Box · 14

Albion · 15

Missing From The Point Of Duty · 16

Turkish · 18

Pattie And Chips And A Can Of Coke · 19

The Black Mill · 20

Stones Thrown Through Me · 21

The Other Foot · 22

Eight Floors Up · 23

Pyrex · 24

Night Shift · 25

I Kissed A Judge And I Liked It · 26

Message From John · 27

Dim · 28

The Last Poem I WIll Ever Write About Sid · 29

Snug · 30

Peer Of The Realm · 31

Banker's Lament · 32

Dear Publisher (For Shane) · 33

The Knowledge · 34

Please Come To Hornsea · 36

Long Arm Of The Law · 37

Brantingham · 38

Terry · 39

Famous · 41

Tiger's Lair · 42

Bare Hands · 43

Held · 44

Incident On King Edward Street · 45

Tat · 46

Pillar Of The Community · 47

Another Terry Poem · 48

Adidas · 49

Holiday · 50

The Return · 51

4 A.M. · 52

Me And My Big Mouth · 53

York · 54

Up · 55

Dawn Chorus · 56

Rhubarb Rhubarb · 57

How D'Ya Like Your Eggs In The Morning · 58

Stephen · 59

Never Stand On A Deckchair · 60

Day Out · 61

Away With The Fairies · 62

SOMETIMES
I'M SO HAPPY
I'M NOT SAFE
ON THE
STREETS

This book is dedicated to Anthony Weilds

MARY

Even though
she once got bitten

by a monkey
on the Rock of Gibraltar

I couldn't fault her

She was beautiful and kind
and didn't even mind

that we never made it
to the bedroom

let alone the altar.

OAK VAULTS

I wasn't staring
at your girlfriend's tits.
I was staring
into space.

I'm the fourth
best poet in Hull
and sometimes the muse
takes me unawares.

I only popped in
for a quiet drink
and to pay homage
to the queens of country.

So loosen your grip
before I let rip
and overpower you
with my poetry.

HULL HATH NO FURY
LIKE A POET SCORNED

I refuse to enter
the East Yorkshire Arts Centre
after someone who works there
said my poems were shit.

Not for all the tea in China
would I degrade myself and enter
the East Yorkshire Arts Centre
after someone who works there
said I was semi-illiterate.

No. I will never ever enter
the East Yorkshire Arts Centre
after someone who works there
said I was many things but not a poet.

I know she's not been well
since her husband ran off with a slag
but taking it out on me
and my wonderful poetry
isn't going to make me give him back.

SID

We're together
because you're brutal
in a gentle way.

We're together
because I spend and spend
and never pay.

We're together
because work takes you overseas
one week in four.

We're together
because that's when I entertain
the men next door.

We're together
because I'm skilled in the art
of covering my tracks.

We're together
because you've had a stroke
and two heart attacks.

We're together
because you worship
the ground I tread.

We're together
because you keep to your
side of the bed.

BAD PENNY

He broke my heart
like it's never

been broken before.
Then one day

when it was
starting to mend

he came back
and broke it some more.

METAL BOX

Meet me
in the long grass
by what's left

of the factory
where our mothers
worked

and I will count
the freckles
on your back

then later
when you're
gone

I'll see
how far I get
with the stars.

ALBION

In The Albion,
spitting distance
from Anne Bronte's grave,

I lost seven games of pool
to a carpet fitter
from Grimsby.

But was I disappointed?
No. In fact, I couldn't
have been happier,

not because he was a fit,
no-nonsense, ex-borstal boy
descendant of Keats,

but because I got to the jukebox first
and made sure for the rest of the night
Patsy Cline took her rightful place.

MISSING FROM THE POINT OF DUTY

Woke up
at twenty past four
with a nosebleed
and morning glory.

On the way to work
saw a man pissing
and two foxes.
The future is medieval.

In the canteen, Danny
the amateur boxer
showed off his latest tattoo
while lads gathered round

a mobile phone
to watch a woman
doing God knows what.
The future is medieval.

Had words with the boss
about a wonky wheel
on my trolley
just as the two Sues

laid into Jesus
for preaching
to the casuals.
The future is medieval.

Got my head bitten off
by a scientist
for dropping a laggy-band
on her doorstep,

picked it up and thought
of the damage
a brick could do to her car.
The future is medieval.

Walked home texting
a broken-hearted ex
with shingles
until I got waylaid

by a man with a sweat patch
on his shirt, the shape
of the crucifixion.
The future is medieval.

TURKISH

I'm here because
my one true love
wised up to me
and showed me the door.

I'm here because
I look half decent
in a dim light
surrounded by art deco.

I'm here because
when I slow down
my breathing, the ceiling
becomes the floor.

I'm here because
every room is blessed
with someone skilled in the art
of banishing sorrow.

PATTIE AND CHIPS
AND A CAN OF COKE

There's been
another stabbing.

This time
at the posh

end of
the street,

behind the burnt
out portakabin.

Luckily he
pulled through,

but only just.

Unlike the other
poor bugger

who breathed his last
in the gutter

outside *In Cod We Trust.*

THE BLACK MILL

These pills are meant
to kill my appetite,
but all they do
is keep me up at night.

So let's get the bus
to Beverley,
I'll take your mind off
your boyfriend's tyranny.

We'll walk hand in hand
across the Westwood;
I'll be Mrs Simpson,
you can be Edward.

And when we get to the black mill
I'll stand on the exact spot,
where the one who stole my ghetto-blaster
declared his undying love.

Then after a drink
and a flutter at the races,
I'll book us into the hotel
opposite St Mary's,

where a soldier once fell
from the roof to his death,
and a white rabbit caught the eye
of a boy who wouldn't forget.

STONES THROWN THROUGH ME

Let me be
your target practice,
your very own John The Baptist.

I'm a lonely boy
with a lonely boy's ways,
in need of a distraction
to keep me sane.

So cover me
in cherry blossom
and watch bruises form
like they're going out of fashion.

It's a funny old world
and it gets funnier
by the second.

I'm highly strung and come
with a lot of baggage,
not to mention a slow-puncture
I've had since the Ice Age.

Let me be
your moving target,
your reason for getting up in the morning.

THE OTHER FOOT

When you were fat
and I was fit
I had you jumping through hoops
and chomping at the bit

but now the boot
is on the other foot
I deserve a good kicking
til I'm bruised and cut

not that I'm kinky
or owt like that
it's just I've been a cunt
and now it's time you paid me back.

EIGHT FLOORS UP

Get to the florist,
I need a bouquet
for Doris.

She was taken
badly at bingo.
I'm ringing

from Infirmary,
the doctor says
it's touch and go.

The view is spectacular.

PYREX

When I'm dead
please respect my wishes
and bury me
with my favourite dishes

the ones I grew up with
that came from
my mother's bottom drawer
in the sixties

white with black snow flakes

that I used to think
would look good in a spaceship
with me on board
travelling to distant galaxies.

NIGHT SHIFT

I was singing
I Believe In Angels
while mopping
the canteen floor

when Mary-Sue
burst in with
a carving knife
and screamed -

When you
see my cunt
of a boyfriend
tell him I'll have his balls.

I KISSED A JUDGE AND I LIKED IT

I woke up disorientated
in a judge's bed
because I tell lies
and I'm easily led.

So let me get comfy
on the safety of your lap
while we resurrect my youth
with your girlfriend's slap.

I was eight-stone four
but now I'm twelve-stone six
and you wonder why
I'm back to my old tricks.

MESSAGE FROM JOHN

Where are you
you fucking slag ?

Get your arse
into gear

and get
round here.

I love you.
Keep it to yourself.

DIM

Dim the light, sweetie.
You know the score.

Dim the light, sweetie.
Disguise every flaw.

The years have not been kind,
as well you know.

So dim the light, sweetie.
Then dim it some more.

THE LAST POEM I WILL EVER WRITE ABOUT SID

I am snuggled up
with my sleepy angel,
he was sixty-three today.

We spent the afternoon
in the pub until a game of dominos
descended into an affray.

To calm ourselves down
we went straight to the bookies
and handed over a weeks pay.

In the taxi home he took
my hand and vowed
he would never ever stray.

After tea we staggered
upstairs and watched England
take on Denmark away.

I've just started whispering
sweet nothings in his ear,
but I'm running out of things to say.

When he's in the land of nod,
I will be slipping into my glad rags
and going out to play.

SNUG

I'm dafter
than him

he's dafter
than me.

We're sat
in White Horse

drinking what
we always drink.

The artist is
wearing slacks

which is always
a good sign.

Halfway through
Rhinestone Cowboy

Carol shouts at us
from the bar -

He's fucking good int he,
I'll book him again.

PEER OF THE REALM

He's a little
bit twisted

and his house
is grade two listed.

He loves his wife
very much

but sometimes
she can't get in touch

because he's on
a sling somewhere

being fisted
by a lady from

Weston-Super-Mare.

BANKER'S LAMENT

My little heart
is filled with despair.
I live in London,
I'm a billionaire.

I work with people
who call me Sir.
I work with people
who wouldn't care

if thugs broke into
my house in Mayfair,
stole my Renoir
and tied me to a chair.

Love, love, love
is everywhere.
When, when, when
will I get my share ?

DEAR PUBLISHER (FOR SHANE)

The next time
I email, text
or call

I'll expect
your mood
to lift not fall.

Your indifference
is a dagger
in my heart.

Your indifference
would crush
Napolean Bonaparte.

The next time
I get in touch
with you

I want you on
your knees sobbing
tears of gratitude.

THE KNOWLEDGE

When I saw
his spiders
web tattoo

I knew
I knew
I knew.

When he leered
at every
passing lass

I knew
I knew
I knew.

When he said
he'd done a stretch
for G.B.H

I knew
I knew
I knew.

When he said
he hated
queers

I knew
I knew
I knew

he'd be back
at mine in the
early hours

teaching me
a thing
or two.

PLEASE COME TO HORNSEA

Hornsea is strange.
Hornsea is bleak.
What it lacks in things to do,
it makes up for in mystique.

Hornsea welcomes everyone
whether straight-laced or a freak.
Hornsea is where
the strong fear the weak.

Please come to Hornsea,
please, please come.
It's nearly as good as Withernsea
and much better than Immingham.

LONG ARM OF THE LAW

In Bluebell Wood
he gave me the third degree,
for singing, *Que sera, sera*
whatever will be, will be.

In Bluebell Wood
he reprimanded me,
for possessing a flask
filled with peppermint tea.

In Bluebell Wood
he cautioned me,
for passing the time of day
with a trucker from Clacton-on-Sea.

In Bluebell Wood
he manhandled me,
for being in awe of Mother Nature
in all her majesty.

In Bluebell Wood
he handcuffed himself to a tree,
and said, *Whatever you do,*
don't be gentle with me.

BRANTINGHAM

A clean living vegan
with no morals, said -

*How deep into the woods
are you taking me ?*

*I've heard the centre
is ablaze with bluebells*

*or would you prefer
the periphery ?*

TERRY

If he hadn't been
bombarded by voices
urging him to stick
a knife in me

I think we could
have made a go of it.

If he hadn't taken
a week off work
to mourn the death
of Mrs Thatcher

I think we could
have made a go of it.

If he hadn't quoted
Richard Littlejohn to me
with a religious fervour
at every opportunity

I think we could
have made a go of it.

If he hadn't thrown up
green bile all over my bed
then gone to the pub
with it caked in his hair

I think we could
have made a go of it.

If he hadn't banged
on and on about how
wonderful George Bush
and Tony Blair were

I think we could
have made a go of it.

If he hadn't swallowed
pill after pill and fell asleep
under a tree on the estate
where my grandma lived

I think we could
have made a go of it.

FAMOUS

I'm suffering
with my back.

I'm in no fit state
for jumping in the sack.

But tell me again
of your days

on the Prinny Ave
meat rack

with You-Know-Who
in his bicycle clips and mac.

TIGER'S LAIR

Phil May is singing
his little heart out

in his black shirt
and black slacks.

His Elvis legs are
all over the place

and the audience
are entranced.

If I had one ounce
of his charisma

I would consider
myself blessed

and if this was
Britain's Got Talent

the golden buzzer
would be pressed.

BARE HANDS

He likes me because
he could destroy me
in seventeen seconds.

He likes me because
I say nowt to no-one
and don't ask any questions.

He likes me because
my hands are small
and his are like shovels.

He likes me because
I love Kate Bush and he makes
hardened men grovel.

He likes me because
I hang on his every word.

He likes me because
I do what he wouldn't dream
of asking his bird.

HELD

Darling
I'm in a lot
of pain,

my star,
my star is on
the wane.

I know it
never did shine
that brightly,

but at least
it shone enough
for strangers

to want to
put their arms
around me.

INCIDENT ON KING EDWARD STREET

I'm sat outside
Nat West

with a can
of coke.

The police have just
carted off a lad

for screaming abuse
at a woman in a burka.

I hope when
she gets home

there's someone
waiting to hold her.

TAT

He went
to sea.

I never did.

He got
a tattoo

when he
was a kid.

Look at
my skin -

pale and
ink free.

He is a
better man

than I'll
ever be.

PILLAR OF THE COMMUNITY

He's nasty
and controlling.

I wish I wasn't falling.

His fat fingers
get me speaking

in tongues.

I'm a house
without a roof,

a ladder
without rungs.

ANOTHER TERRY POEM

When I see a can
of Strongbow

I think of you
my dear.

When I see
a pool of sick

on the pavement

I think of you
my dear.

When I see a man
pissing in a doorway

I think of you
my dear.

When I'm sat
in The Minerva

I think of your
hand in mine
on the pier.

ADIDAS

Please don't mucky my trainers
they cost me an afternoon
in Earl's Court
with a stand up comedian

and it's best we don't linger
too long here,
pigs have a talent
for getting away with murder.

We'll be better off
in the elephant's graveyard
where the punters are well heeled
and the bar staff turn a blind eye

and come closing
we can wait outside
with the other lads
and peer into cars

as they slowly pass.

HOLIDAY

We are only
four miles from Filey
and I am distantly related
to Dorothy Squires

and your father
played football
in the forties
for Doncaster Rovers.

And last night on the beach
while the sea had a fit
you caressed
and I bit.

Then later on
in bed watching telly
you fell asleep in my arms
and it felt like I belonged.

But now let's go to where
Butlins once stood
I went there every year
a long time ago.

And when we get back
I'll rake out some photos taken there,
of me, my mam and dad
and my little sister.

THE RETURN

On the 19th July 1977
a plane touched down
from Pakistan
at Heathrow Airport
and a man
with everything to declare
passed unnoticed through customs

4 A.M.

I'm not frightened,
but I should be.

I am watching
things happen.

I go where
the fancy takes me.

This is how it is,
how it should be.

Smile sweetly,
breathe deeply.

Twenty pounds
is a lot of money.

ME AND MY BIG MOUTH

Doncaster John
has got a gun
and he wants to blow
my head off.

I told him he had
the wrong end of the stick
but he wouldn't listen
to reason.

I begged his wife
and I begged his mam
to tell him I said nowt
to no one.

They said they'd try
and make him see sense
but told me not to build
my hopes up.

Doncaster John
has got a gun
and it looks like my days
are numbered.

YORK

Don't wear
white trousers

down Dame
Judi Dench Walk.

I know someone
who did

and they ended up
in a coma.

UP

As I walked past
Poundstretcher Extra

I caught a glimpse
of my reflection

and for once wasn't
repulsed by what I saw.

In fact, I felt that good
about myself,

I threw my cap into the air
like Mary Tyler Moore.

DAWN CHORUS

There's a pissed up librarian
at the foot of my bed
massaging my feet
and singing *The World Is A Circle.*

I only invited him back
because from certain angles
he has the look of Craig the builder
from *Big Brother 2000.*

Up to now he's been
the perfect gentleman
and if it wasn't for my stretch marks
I'd let him massage somewhere else.

I don't know when he's leaving
and I'm reluctant to ask
in case he takes offence
and ransacks my home.

If anything were to happen
to my Art Deco teapots
and Alan Minter memorabilia
the shock would haunt me for the rest of my days.

RHUBARB RHUBARB

I once met
an Emmerdale extra
on a bench above the bogs
by Queen Victoria.

I think his name was Martin
but I could be wrong.
He was skinny and wore glasses
that made his eyes look big.

We met up a week later
on the bridge by The Deep
and walked along the river
to his flat near where Wilberforce lived.

Considering he was a theatrical,
he didn't say much.
Not even when I grilled him
for any gossip on the cast.

And when I mentioned
I'd been watching since
nineteen seventy two,
he looked at me like I needed help.

That was the last time
I saw him in the flesh,
and I've not seen him in *The Woolpack*
since I don't know when.

HOW D'YA LIKE YOUR
EGGS IN THE MORNING?

All the builders
in the B&B

are watching
the match highlights

on Sky Sports 3

apart from the prettiest
who's been watching me

since I sang along with
the Tropicana advert

rather too
enthusiastically.

STEPHEN

I want to go
to Withernsea,
with my pal who sees
the good in me.

I think he needs
his eyes testing,
but that's
another story.

I don't care
how we get there,
as long as
it's by bus.

We'll sit on
the top deck,
and invoke the gods
of Holderness.

NEVER STAND ON A DECKCHAIR

Never stand on a deckchair.
No. Never stand on a deckchair.
A friend of mine once did
and it collapsed beneath her.
It collapsed beneath her.

Never stand on a deckchair.
No. Never stand on a deckchair.
A friend of mine once did
and now she's only got one little finger.
Only one little finger.

Never stand on a deckchair.
No. Never stand on a deckchair.
A friend of mine once did
and now she's got a phobia.
A terrible phobia.

And all because on a whim
she decided to give her hanging basket a trim.
So. Please, please, please beware
and never, ever, ever, ever
stand on a deckchair.

DAY OUT

In Bridlington today
the waves were crashing,
the cliffs were golden
and I made a man
with an erection tut.

In Bridlington today
I had a sweat on at bingo
and bought a black jersey
from a charity shop.

In Bridlington today
I had my tea in
The Hook And Parrot
and nearly got hit
in the head by a dart.

In Bridlington today
I sat on a bench
and let a wind turbine
break my heart.

AWAY WITH THE FAIRIES

Sometimes I'm a shrinking violet.
Sometimes I'm a diva.
Sometimes I'm in control.
Sometimes I get full moon fever.

Sometimes I'm so happy
I'm not safe on the streets.
Sometimes I'm a beautiful young woman
in a tight blue top and matching skirt with pleats.

Sometimes I watch the world go by
from the comfort of my favourite chair.
Sometimes I venture outside
and do things decent men wouldn't dare.

Sometimes I'm a clinically obese
Elvis impersonator with Tourette's
seeking an understanding lady
for walks in the country and kinky sex.

Sometimes I see God in the eyes
of my favourite bingo caller.
Sometimes I'm a grain of sand
on the beach at Brid, only smaller.

Dean Wilson would like to thank:

Jim and Julie Orwin, John Citizen, Tim Wells, Peter Knaggs (Best Poet in Hull), Michael Mackmin, Joanna Cutts, Niall O'Sullivan, Daithidh MacEochaidh, Edward Barker, Dai Parsons, Nicholas Bielby, Philip Barnes (R.I.P.), Daphne Glazer, Jean Hartley (R.I.P.), Julia Bird, Jody Porter, Roddy Lumsden, Fiona Curran, Jonathan and Glynn, Paul Lyalls, Bruce Woodcock, Phill Hutchinson, Julie Corbett, Ruth Getz, Laura O'Donnel, Nicky Ellam, Michelle Dee, Dave Lee, Chris Holder, Joe Hakim, Dave Windass, Steve Dearden, Jim Higo, Miki Higgins, Mike Watts, Kev, Stephen Deas, Robin Lee, Phil May, Graham Scott, Ellie Grice, Martin King, Sam Tobin, Anna Goodall, Nathan Penlington, John Bush, Rob Eunson, Bryan and Jim forever, Paul and Dean and Sid.

This book will be my undoing.
I blame Russ Litten and Shane Rhodes.

Some of these poems first appeared in the following publications:

Rising, Pennine Platform, The Shop, Morning Star, The Wolf, Pen Pusher Magazine, South Bank Poetry, Smiths Knoll, Hanging Johnny, The Slab, Magma, The Fix, Limelight, The Reater and The Hull Collection.

Also by Dean Wilson:

There Are Worse Things I Could Do Than Write A Poem Or Two (Chapbook)

Published by Dancing Sisters.